IRISH AMERICANS

Emigration to the New World

There are some forty million Irish Americans in the United States of America, descendants of those who, over the past four centuries, crossed the Atlantic in successive waves of emigrations.

Life in America was rarely easy and many of the new immigrants fell by the wayside; but eventually they achieved a standard of living unimaginable in the world they had left behind. Over the generations they rose to the highest positions in politics, the labour movement, the professions, industry, commerce and the arts, and their very numbers made them a powerful political force.

Yet more than any other ethnic group, the Irish nurture a great nostalgia for the Emerald Isle', their ancestral homeland. *The Irish Americans* offers an introduction to the world of their ancestors and, perhaps, their own roots.

Roots: The Ulster Scots

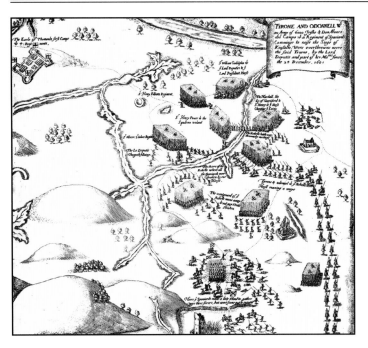

During the reign of Elizabeth I England became staunchly Protestant, with the Queen as Supreme Head of the Church, and Catholics were regarded as sympathetic to her traditional enemies – France and Spain, both Catholic countries, as was Ireland. The latter had never been completely subdued and most of the land was still owned by the Gaelic lords, descendants of the Irish kings and the Old English, whose roots went back to the Anglo-Norman invasion of the 12th century and whose loyalties were divided between the English crown, their Catholic faith and the supremacy of the Pope. Their ultimate interest, however, lay in the preservation of their estates and wealth.

Elizabeth rightly suspected that the Catholic Irish were quite capable of letting England's enemies in by the back door. To counter this threat, a policy of plantation was adopted whereby land was taken from Catholics and given to Protestants who would be loyal to the crown and the established church, and would defend their land against any Catholic uprising, Irish or invading. Partly by force and partly by negotiation Elizabeth managed plantations in the provinces of Munster and Monaghan; but in Ulster, the northern Irish lords still ruled, and in 1594 O'Neill, Earl of Tyrone and O'Donnell, Earl of Tyrconnell, declared war on the English. However, the untrained Irish forces had little hope of success

...ainst the stronger and better-armed ...nglish; a Spanish fleet that came to their ...d in 1601 was immediately besieged and ...on forced to surrender. By 1603 it was ...l over, and the great O'Neill submitted.

The Queen had died three days ...rlier, and his submission was to a more ...mpathetic James I who allowed him ...d his allies to return to live on their ...tates, but as landlords under the crown ...d without their ancient titles or power. ...he Gaelic laws, customs and language ...ere replaced by government from ...ublin, and English common law and ...nguage. Four years later the Earls and ...o followers fled secretly to the Conti-...nt; this was judged to be treason, and ...eir estates were forfeited to the crown.

James I seized the opportunity to ...dulge in plantation on a grand scale. ...he Catholic populations of the six coun-...es of Armagh, Cavan, Coleraine, Tyrone, ...onegal and Fermanagh were segregated ...reservations and the vacant land ...nded over to Protestant landlords and ...nants. Most of the new tenantry were ...wland Scots whom James, who was also ...mes VI of Scotland, invited to settle in ...lster. During the 17th century, the Ulster ...ots made the province the most indus-...ous in Ireland, and Belfast a city with ...e world's largest shipyards, linen mills, ...undries and tobacco factories.

A change in their fortunes began in ...90 when William of Orange landed ...Carrickfergus to defeat James II's ...atholic Irish and French army at the ...ttle of the Boyne. At the subsequent ...eaty of Limerick, William granted ...ligious freedom to Ireland; but the

Protestant Irish parliament introduced instead Penal Laws intended to outlaw the Catholic faith. They also circum-scribed dissenters, and the Ulster Scots, as Presbyterians, were dissenters. They were debarred from holding office under the crown, marriages by their ministers were not recognised, and they had to pay fines if they did not attend Church of Ireland services, while at the same time having to pay tithes to the established church and support their own ministers. They were also debarred from owning freehold land; they could only obtain leases, with rents that increased on renewal. They had no love for land they could not own, so in their thousands they sold their leases and their stock and set sail for America where they could worship as they wanted to, buy land cheaply, be their own masters and owe no man.

ABOVE:
Following the defeat of his Catholic Irish and French army in 1690, James II slipped away to France, where he died in exile.

BELOW:
The Irish uprising at the close of the 16th century ended in the Earl of Tyrone's 'false' submission to James I; four years later Tyrone left Ireland for ever.

Ulster Scots in America

RIGHT:
A new settlement in a forest clearing in north-west America, one of many established by the pioneering Ulster Scots in the 18th century.

BELOW:
A family would walk hundreds of miles beside their Conestoga wagon, which contained everything they needed to establish a foothold in the wilderness.

he population of the English colonies in America in 1700 was no more than 250,000, a figure which was to rise in the next 50 years to about one million. This growth was helped not only by the influx of a further 250,000 from Ulster, but also by the remarkable fertility of the early colonists, among whom families of 20 children were not uncommon. The new immigrants from Ulster found the land around the ports already densely

populated and, of necessity, had to press on inland into the difficult territory of the Appalachian back country.

Their parents had been pioneers in Ireland, and they were determined not to be denied a second time. They became the frontiersmen of colonial America, pushing out the boundaries of the New World which had remained virtually static for nearly a hundred years. They cleared the forests to make their farms and fortified them with stockades. But they also took with them into the wild country a love of their religion and of learning, so they built churches and schools wherever they went and founded the first American college, a log building in Neshaminy in Pennsylvania.

In a country where land was more or less free for the asking, no man would work for another when he could have his own farm, so to find hired hands was impossible; a man needed a wife and children in order to prosper. Girls were encouraged to marry young, and single women were rare; widows with children were eagerly sought after, for every child provided an extra pair of hands.

At the beginning of the 18th century settlers headed west on foot with their belongings carried on packhorses or mules; then came the Conestoga wagon,

hich originated in Pennsylvania and
ecame the standard vehicle for those on
he wagon trails. By the 1770s there were
23 Ulster settlements and, as Benjamin
ranklin remarked: 'They are in a fair way
o taking over the state.' They were not
ivided in their loyalty between the old
ountry and the new, and were the first
o declare for independence when they
dopted the Mecklenburg Resolution of
ndependence at a convention of Scotch-
rish, as they were by then known. The
ctual Declaration of Independence on
 July 1776, which signalled the birth of
he American nation, had among its
ignatories five men of Ulster stock, as
vas the Secretary of Congress; so too were
nany of the generals and half the troops
n the ensuing War of Independence.

The war over, they reverted to their
ole of pioneers; looking west along
he wilderness road, they crossed the
Appalachian Mountains through the
Cumberland Gap to enter the Blue Grass
ountry of Kentucky and Tennessee,
nence on to the great central basin of
America and the Pacific coast. But while
nany were opening up the continent,
thers were gaining the heights in politics

'A grim stern people, strong and simple, powerful for good and evil, swayed by the gusts of stormy passion, the love of freedom rooted in their very hearts' core… They suffered terrible injuries at the hands of the red men, and on their foes they waged a terrible warfare in return. They were relentless, revengeful, suspicious, knowing neither ruth nor pity; they were also upright, resolute and fearless, loyal to their friends, and devoted to their country. In spite of their many failings, they were of all men the best fitted to conquer the wilderness and hold it against all comers.'

PRESIDENT THEODORE ROOSEVELT

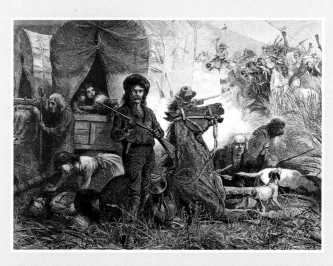

and becoming leaders in all walks of life.
They and their descendants were to
produce ten Presidents of the United
States occupying the White House for
56 years in a period of 92 years.

ABOVE:
The pioneers' progress
through the wild back country was often hampered by
Red Indian attack on their
wagon trains and camps.

LEFT:
The skill of linen production
was carried over from
Ulster; parties often devel-
oped when neighbours gathered for flax scutching.

The Irish Potato Famine

RIGHT:
The failure of the potato harvest in 1846 marked the end of a long struggle by many families to survive on a diet of potatoes and milk.

A rapidly rising population in Ireland at the end of the 18th century led to the exploitation of the land and rising rents. In the countryside as a whole, half of all farms were under 5 acres. With the end of the Napoleonic Wars in 1815, the demand for Irish grain fell dramatically as Britain again imported from the Continent. At the same time, with the growth of industrial towns in England, the market for meat increased, so landlords began to convert their land from tillage to pasture, thus reducing the need for farm labourers. While linen manufacture had remained a cottage industry, spinning women could supplement the family income; but by 1830 this work was being taken over by mechanised mills using a fraction of the labour. Consequently the larger part of the population was unemployed.

Fortunately there was an abundance of the cheapest food, the potato, which together with milk provided a surprisingly nutritious diet. As the population rose, however, so did the scramble for land; holdings were divided to provide as little as half an acre for a family to grow enough potatoes on which to survive. Landlords demanded exorbitant rents, and many a smallholder paid excessively for land because the alternative was to take to the road and beg. The more prosperous farmers sold up and emigrated, starting an exodus that was to last throughout the 1800s.

DESTITUTION IN IRELAND.— FAILURE OF THE POTATO CROP

RIGHT:
The starving tenants, unable to pay their rents, were often evicted and their homes pulled down to 'encourage' them to emigrate.

In 1844 reports came from America that a mysterious disease had attacked their potato crop. Scant attention was paid to them; but in September the crops started perishing around Dublin, and by the end of the month rotting potatoes were being harvested countrywide. Thousands of wretched peasants were obliged to eat the poisonous mess for want of any other food; this led to an epidemic of dysentry and other fevers which, coupled with sheer starvation, were to kill some million souls in four years.

Governmental response to the tragedy was abysmal; it was the age of *laissez-faire*, when no government intervention should threaten private enterprise or property. When the cost of other food threatened to rise too high, a quantity of Indian corn was imported from America to hold prices down; however, not only was it insufficient, but those few who received this 'bounty' neither liked it nor knew how to cook it and, furthermore, no practical means existed for its fair distribution.

The failure was even greater in 1846, and in 1847 gales and snow added to the misery. Workhouses and hastily arranged fever hospitals were filled to overflowing. Aid from America and relief work by private agencies, particularly the Quakers, was meritorious but inadequate. The landlords were getting no rents from their starving tenants, so in turn could not pay the rates to support the Poor Law system which had been extended to Ireland in 1834. The workhouses set in motion a programme of forced emigration known as 'shovelling out'. Workhouses and landlords alike found it cheaper to pay passages or even to charter ships than to continue supporting whole populations of destitute peasants. Even so a third of all landlords were ruined and forced to sell their estates. Many of the new owners were English and Scotch and, in order to consolidate their farms and improve their new estates, they cleared the land of smallholdings and cottages – so the evictions continued. For the dispossessed, there were but two alternatives – to beg or to emigrate.

ABOVE:
Gangs of demolition men were employed by the landlords; they could destroy as many as 30 houses in a morning.

ABOVE:
The fine-looking potatoes that were harvested collapsed into fetid blobs.

BELOW:

BELOW:

A Passengers' Contract Ticket to New York, issued to Mary Oats by Tapscott's American Emigration Office, of Liverpool and Dublin, in March 1857. The cost of the voyage in steerage aboard the ship *West Point* was £4.2s.6d. The ticket is on display in the Merseyside Maritime Museum, Liverpool.

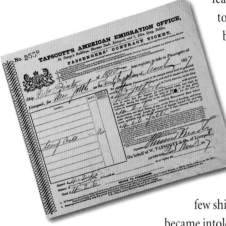

RIGHT:

A detail from the painting *The Emigrants* by Erskine Nicol. A scene such as this, of a young couple with their few possessions tied into bundles, would have been typical during the Irish potato famine.

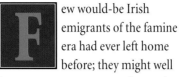

Few would-be Irish emigrants of the famine era had ever left home before; they might well have never seen a town or the sea, let alone a ship. They had no sense of geography, and they could neither read nor write. As they started off walking to the coast, they were venturing into the unknown from which there would be no return. It must have been fearful; but greater fears were to come, and hardship as bad as that from which they were escaping.

In the period before and early on during the great famine, emigration to America was totally disorganised and, with too many wanting to board too few ships, the overcrowding became intolerable. Emigrants sailed in whatever ships would take them for the little money they had; some were small merchant vessels suitable only for coastal trade, and passengers were at the mercy of the captains, most of whom regarded them more as cargo than as humans. The staple rations were often little more than meal, biscuits and brackish water, and those who did not bring extra provisions of their own arrived in America emaciated and weak with hunger. In rough weather they were battened down in the darkness below decks, without ventilation, to lie two or three to a 16 inch-wide bunk, vomiting over themselves and each other; with lack of food, insanitary conditions and seasickness, typhus and cholera were common and often fatal. The ships' doctors often refused to descend into the fetid depths of the hold, or insisted on the sick coming on deck for treatment.

By the time of the potato famine, three-quarters of all Irish emigrants to America were travelling via Liverpool, the main British port for the transatlantic trade. The emigrants crossed from Irish ports to Liverpool by small packet boats, mainly used for carrying cattle to the mainland. They went as deck cargo, often several hundred jammed together in the open with no shelter, while the cattle, being more valuable, were housed

n stalls under cover. English ships plying the Atlantic brought timber, flax, tobacco and grain from America; but there was little trade the other way, and so it was very profitable to erect temporary bunks in the cargo holds and fill them with emigrants. A family, unless very large, would be allocated only one berth with perhaps two feet of headroom between bunks.

After 1847 the emigrant trade out of Liverpool came to be dominated by the

'The desire to reach America being exceeding strong, many of the emigrants are content to submit to very great hardship during the voyage.'

EARL GREY, SECRETARY OF STATE FOR THE COLONIES

LEFT:
This tableau of emigrants experiencing the miseries of a storm at sea is in the Cobh Heritage Centre, Co Cork.

Americans who were building big packet boats specifically designed to carry large numbers in steerage. Conditions on board were marginally better than on the much smaller sailing ships; and with the coming of the steamship, crossing in steerage became more bearable because, although unpleasant, it lasted seven to ten days rather than four to seven weeks. At first only the more affluent could afford to travel by steamer, the fares starting at about 8 guineas as against £3 in steerage on a sailing ship. With plenty of steam for heating and cooking, they offered more comfort and regular hot food. Demand soon brought the price of fares down and by 1856 over 5,000 emigrants had reached New York under steam; by 1868 three-quarters of all Atlantic crossings were by steamer.

ABOVE:
Emigrants of all ages gather together on the quay at Cork, ready to begin their long and arduous journey to the New World.

ABOVE:
Many of those who emigrated to escape the famine were uneducated and unskilled; they worked as labourers, building new roads and railways.

RIGHT:
The chief Democratic Party in New York was run from Tammany Hall. These were the days of 'boss' politics, whereby favours were granted in return for a vote. Under 'Honest' John Kelly, many social services were provided for Irish American constituents.

Unlike the emigrants out of Ulster in the 18th century, the four million emigrants to America in the 19th century were largely destitute, in poor health, illiterate and unskilled. They left a rural society, but had no knowledge of farming; and for many there was no choice but to find low-paid work in the cities, humping, heaving and digging for a living, while the womenfolk ended up as servants or as sweated labour in the mills. To compound their problems, poor pay condemned them to live in unhealthy crowded slums where they suffered the highest infant mortality in the country.

They survived because they were prolific breeders; but it was the second and third generations who were to reap the benefits of life in an increasingly industrial and affluent America. It was Irish muscle power that built the roads, railways, canals and expanding cities of America during the second half of the 19th century. For a long time they were looked down on by the Protestant 'Yankee' establishment as ignoramuses, fit only for near-slave labour. This attitude provoked them into organising themselves in defence of their rights, often their lives; they became the pioneers of the labour unions, and before the end of the century more than half the presidents of the unions and the American Federation of Labor were first or second generation Irish-Americans. At the same time their very numbers were to give them political clout in the cities, and the 1870s saw them in control of municipal politics in Boston, Chicago, St Louis and San Francisco.

More than 200,000 Irishmen fought in the Civil War of the 1860s, most of them on the Unionist side. Their prowess in the army and their loyalty to the

Unionist cause somewhat alleviated the contempt in which the first famine immigrants had been held. The years immediately after the Civil War saw enormous economic growth in the newly united States, which in turn created an increasing demand for labour. This

demand, combined with remittances home from immigrants who had begun to earn and save, fuelled a new emigrant movement out of Ireland. Meanwhile the Irish immigrants and their children were starting to climb the social ladder and to acquire professional and technical qualifications. Around the turn of the century a further two million Irish arrived in America, their transition eased by the steam ship, and their arrival welcomed by the numerous Irish associations and societies that had come into being.

They no longer had to worry about being looked upon as second-class citizens – by their very numbers they were already a power in the land – and each year on 17 March they showed their pride in their homeland by the St Patrick's Day parade. In modern times it takes three hours for this parade to pass City Hall in New York. Nor were they now the lowest-paid menial workers; immigrants from Italy and eastern Europe had taken over that role. From local politics they had moved into Congress and the Senate, and at the turn of the century the Democratic party machine was firmly in Irish hands. Finally in 1960 one of their number became the first Catholic Irish American President of the USA.

ABOVE:
A cartoon illustrating the low regard in which the Irish were held in the mid 19th century.

LEFT:
Letters from America urged relations in Ireland to emigrate.

BELOW:
The famous Fighting 69th of New York, an all-Irish regiment commanded by Thomas Meagher, who became a brigadier-general and Governor of Montana.

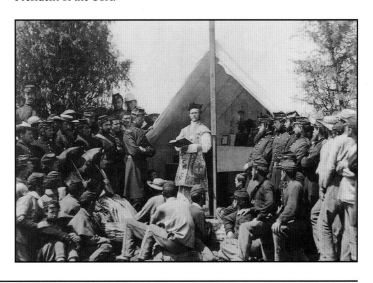

The numbers in the Heritage Trail cross refer to the map on the inside front cover.

Of the 15 Presidents of the United States of Irish ancestry, 12 hailed from the province of Ulster, and three of those were first generation Americans. Presidents Truman and Eisenhower have also made tentative claims to having some Ulster blood. As a result, the people of Northern Ireland have shown a fine regard for their American connections, and have located and renovated or rebuilt several presidential ancestral homes, as well as those of a number of other prominent Americans.

The first of the first generation American presidents was **Andrew Jackson** (1827–37); he was conceived in Co Antrim, but the emigrant ship got his mother across the Atlantic in time for him to be born on American soil in 1767. His parents' home in Boneybefore 17, near the ferry terminal at Larne 11, which was rebuilt and occupied as a farmhouse until 1970, has been put back to its original state with earth floor and open turf fire, and furnished as it would have been in their time. His life story as lawyer, congressman, senator, judge, Indian fighter and major-general is told in words and pictures inside the cottage.

At Dreen by Cullybackey 9 is the little cottage that was the home of the parents of **Chester Alan Arthur**, who became 21st President of the USA in 1881. It has been restored by the National Trust and furnished as a typical 19th-century farmstead.

The Wilson farmstead in Co Tyrone, a little way out of Strabane at Dergalt 14 on the Plumstead road, is the best preserved of all the homes, and one may well be shown round by a member of the same Wilson family who still farm the surrounding land. The house, where **President Woodrow Wilson**'s grandfather lived, is furnished as it was in the early 19th century, and is one of the best examples to be seen of an 18th/early 19th-century farmhouse. The main room was the kitchen, and the point around which the life of the house revolved was the open turf fire. Here old customs were observed and *ceilidhs* were held. The second floor was reached by a ladder,

RIGHT:
The ancestral home of Chester Alan Arthur, 21st President of the USA, has been restored by the National Trust.

BELOW:
The story of Andrew Jackson, the first of the first generation American presidents, is portrayed in the cottage where his parents lived.

visitors. The half-door entrance has a jamb wall just inside; this is a free-standing draught screen to protect the interior, especially the peat fire, and is typical of Ulster houses of the time. The floors are of puddled clay, hard wearing and easily repaired. Above the open fire is a half loft with bed and storage space reached by a ladder.

out in later times a fixed staircase was installed to an opening in the upper floor. Another room had two beds which could be curtained off during the day if it was being used for weddings, wakes or visitors. The beams and A-frames are cut from bog oak, and under the thatch a layer of sods form insulation; the walls are rough whitewashed stone. Senior members of the family slept in the warmth of the kitchen in an out-shot, a recess near the fire projecting outwards from the wall of the house to give it breadth. The house was occupied by the Wilsons until it was taken over and renovated by the National Trust.

The father of **President James Buchanan** (1857–61) emigrated from the ancestral home at Deroran 24 near Omagh, Co Tyrone, and the President was born in a log cabin in Franklin County in 1791.

Another interesting little house in Co Tyrone is the home of **Ulysses Simpson Grant**'s grandfather, a two-roomed cottage dating from 1600 at Dergina 29, a little way off the Belfast-Fermanagh road. During restoration, sections of an original earth wall reinforced with reed were exposed and are now visible to

On the main Belfast-Enniskillen road is the little town of Augher 28 and next door is the village of Glenhoy where **John Joseph Hughes**, the first Catholic Archbishop of New York, was born in 1797. It was he who built St Patrick's Cathedral on Fifth Avenue. The house in which he lived as a boy has been removed and rebuilt in the Ulster American Folk Park at Camphill near Omagh, but there is a memorial window to him in St McCartan's Church at Ballynagurragh just a mile south of Augher. The Hughes family were weavers and their farm was given over to flax. One of the rooms housed a loom on which in winter they made linen.

BELOW:
This tiny stone outbuilding is all that remains of the ancestral home of the Kennedy family; their story is told at the Kennedy Centre, New Ross.

Just over the border into Donegal at Lifford 13, near Strabane, Cavanacors House, built in 1600, was the home of **Captain Robert Polk** who emigrated to Maryland about 1860 with his wife, a Miss Tasker, also from Strabane. His great great great grandson, **James Knox Polk**, became the 11th US President (1845–49).

This may be a disappointment to the many Americans who visit it; but a new Kennedy Centre has been opened in New Ross 47 nearby from where his great grandfather emigrated. Apart from telling the Kennedy story, it claims that anybody whose ancestors sailed to Ellis Island in New York from any part of Ireland or Liverpool between 1848 and 1925 can trace them through its database. A grander memorial to the late President is the John F. Kennedy Arboretum. Extending to 252 hectares, with 4,500 trees and shrubs from all over the world, it lies at the foot of Slievecoilta, a 271m hill south of New Ross. A motor road runs to the summit, from which six counties of Ireland can be seen on a clear day. The project was initiated with financial help from American citizens of Irish origin, and is now run by the Irish Forestry Board.

BELOW:
The birth and baptismal certificate of President Ronald Reagan's great-grandfather, who emigrated first to England, and then, in 1858, to America.

The **Kennedy** ancestral home still stands in the tiny village of Dunganstown 48, but is now no more than an unimpressive stone outbuilding at the entrance to a farm occupied by Mary Anne Ryan, a cousin of the late President.

Taking the main road west from Waterford to Clonmel, and then minor roads, you arrive at Ballyporeen 51, the ancestral village of **President Reagan**. The family house was pulled down at the time that Ireland joined the Common Market when, in a spirit of optimism, many small farms were amalgamated into larger units; the Reagan cottage stood in the way. However, the village does have a Ronald Reagan Centre which tells the story of his visit by helicopter on 3 June 1984 when he was shown the register in which was recorded the baptism of his great grandfather in the Church of the Assumption in 1829; and there is now a public house named after him.

Birth and Baptismal Certificate

Diocese of...... Waterford & Lismore....... Parish of...... Ballyporeen.......
On examination of the Register of Baptisms of above Parish I certify that according to it...... Michael Regan......
was born on............day of...... no record......, and was baptised according to the Rites of the Catholic Church on...3....day of...September 1829....in the Church of...the Assumption Ballyporeen...by the Rev...Martin Redmond.
Parents...... Thomas Regan (Doolis)...... Margaret Murphy......
Sponsors...... William Regan...... Catherine Walsh......
Confirmed...no record.... Married...no record....
Signed...Fr Fanna Condon P.P. C.C.
Given this...26...day of...February 81...at...
...Ballyporeen...... Cahir, Co. Tipperary, Ireland.

L.S.

VERITAS CO. LTD. DUBLIN

The story of the Ulster American Folk Park at Camphill 22, Co Tyrone, starts in 1813 when Thomas Mellon was born in the cottage which still stands at its centre. When he was five years old his parents sold their 23-acre farm for 200 guineas – a small fortune at that time – and emigrated to America. The 90-day voyage was a trauma about which Thomas had 'no desire to speak' for the rest of his life. He became rich and powerful as the founder of the Mellon Bank and as a judge. The site around the cottage now covers 60 acres and tells the story of how men and women lived in Ulster and in the New World. Buildings have been transported from all over the province and re-erected, and log dwellings constructed in facsimile of those that the pioneer immigrants built in America. The visitor can wander in and out of the forge, the Meeting House, the schoolhouse and the authentic houses of the Mellon and Hughes families. Then boarding a life-size section of a ship one is 'transported' to the New World. All the buildings contain authentic furniture, cooking utensils and other implements, and costumed staff enact the life and work of blacksmith, school teacher, weaver, spinner and candlemaker. There is an audio-visual exhibition and an extensive library for historical study. Not only is it a place of education and fascination, but an escape from the real world and real time outside.

The Ulster Folk and Transport Museum at Cultra 21 outside Belfast,

LEFT:
The home of the Hughes family, one of many buildings which have been transported from all over the province of Ulster and re-erected with authentic furnishings at the Ulster American Folk Park.

although not directly concerned with emigration, also has a number of buildings and other exhibits which give a hands-on insight into life in the 18th and 19th centuries in Northern Ireland.

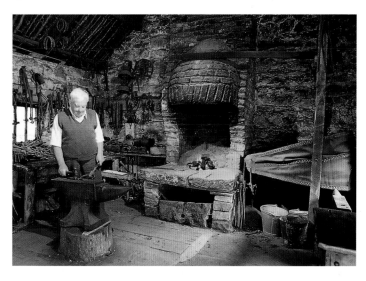

The biggest heritage centre in the Republic is at Cobh 55. A small town in Cork harbour, it was for millions of Irish the last view they had of their homeland as they sailed away to the New World. It grew from a village at the time of the American War of Independence when convoys of ships gathered in the sheltered waters of the harbour before sailing for America with men and materials of war. After that it became a major emigration

ABOVE:
The story of the lives of the Irish emigrants is told at the Ulster American Folk Park; here, the life and work of the blacksmith is re-enacted in the forge.

ABOVE:
The Pennsylvania log farm-house of the Mellon family, at the Ulster American Folk Park. The cottage in which Thomas Mellon, founder of the Mellon Bank, was born still stands at the centre of the park.

RIGHT:
At the height of the potato famine, Liverpool was the main British port for the transatlantic trade. Lodging houses such as these offered spartan hospitality to emigrants waiting for a ship.

port for sailing ships and then for steamers up to the 1920s. In part of the railway station, where would-be emigrants arrived from all over the country, the Cobh Heritage Foundation has created an exhibition called The Queenstown Story. Queenstown is the name which Cove (of Cork) or Cobh was given after a visit by Queen Victoria. It has since reverted to its true Irish name. The exhibition covers

the era of sailing and steam emigration ships and the great liners which called in there before the days of transatlantic flying. The highlights of this presentation are the horribly realistic tableaux of life below decks on a coffin ship, and a huge cinema screen in a darkened hall on which a great square rigger battles with a never ending storm in the Atlantic. The sound of the wind and the crashing breakers is quite deafening, but it is the sound that so frightened the poor emigrants battened down in the dark.

In the far west of Ireland at Corofin 42, on the edge of the limestone Burren with its subterranean lakes, there is a church which has been converted to house a small museum and heritage centre covering the period 1800–1860. The important aspect of this centre is its computerised records of emigrants from Co Clare and the surrounding area during that period.

A new theme park has recently opened at Knockfierna Hill in west Limerick to mark the 150th anniversary

of the 1845 famine. It occupies a site where a community of 1,000 left their homes to look for food; the clay ridges where they grew potatoes are still visible on the hillside.

Lastly, there is the prize-winning Famine Museum occupying the stables of Strokestown 38 Park House, an 18th-century gentleman farmer's estate. It is almost entirely textual with display panels telling the story of the famine, based on Strokestown archives, and of Major Denis Mahon, owner of the estate, who was assassinated when he attempted to evict two-thirds of his starving tenants. There are artefacts such as Notices to Quit and appealing letters from dispossessed tenantry. It is more a student's museum than an entertaining one, and a sad place from which to leave this part of the heritage trail.

As a third of Irish emigrants to America went first to Liverpool and took ship from there, the keen student of this period should visit the Merseyside Maritime Museum in the city's Albert Dock. It has a section devoted to 'Emigrants to a New World' using models and graphics. While waiting for a ship, the emigrants had to run the gauntlet of gangs of runners offering to carry their luggage and find them lodgings. But their real object was to fleece their quarry of what little money and goods they had. The evil practices of these men, the lodging-house keepers and unscrupulous shipping agents is well detailed in the museum. It is particularly well endowed with models and paintings of ships including many that were in the emigrant trade; its archive department, which the public may use, is possibly the best on the subject.

ABOVE:
The story of transatlantic sailing is told at the Cobh Heritage Centre.

ABOVE:
An eviction notice dated 1849, from the collection of famine memorabilia on display at the Famine Museum at Strokestown.

LEFT:
A tableau from the exhibition *Emigrants to the New World* at the Merseyside Maritime Museum in Liverpool.

ANTRIM [19]

Alexander Irvine, who became a missionary in The Bowery, New York, lived here in a picturesque cottage in a back alley called Pogue's Entry.

ARMAGH [31]

The county town and ecclesiastical capital of Ireland, with Catholic and Protestant cathedrals both dedicated to **St Patrick**. The city has an Observatory and Planetarium where the American astronauts **Neil Armstrong** and **James B. Irwin**, both of Ulster stock, are featured in a moon display.

BALLINASCARTHY, Co Cork [57]

The birthplace of **Henry Ford** (1863–1947), founder of the Ford Motor Company in America.

BALLYCLARE, Co Antrim [16]

Believed to have been the ancestral home of **Mark Twain** (1835–1910), the American humourist best known for *Tom Sawyer* and *Huckleberry Finn*; he was born Samuel Clemens. The grandfather of **President Andrew Johnson** (1865–69) lived here briefly with his new bride before emigrating in about 1750.

BALLYCONNEELY, Co Galway [40]

Alcock and **Brown** landed here in 1919 after the first successful transatlantic flight.

BALLYMONEY, Co Londonderry [3]

Home town of the grandfather of **Edgar Allan Poe** (1809–1849), writer and poet.

BANBRIDGE, Co Down [30]

Birthplace in 1796 of **Captain Francis Crozier** who found the North-West Passage in 1848. His monument depicts the expedition ships *Erebus* and *Terror* locked in ice.

THE BIRCHES, Co Antrim [27]

A fenland area near Lough Neagh and the ancestral home of **Thomas J. 'Stonewall' Jackson** (1824–1863), a General on the southern side in the Civil War.

BRANDON BAY, Co Kerry on the Dingle Peninsula [52]

St Brendan and his crew set sail across the Atlantic from here in the 6th century.

BROUGHSHANE, Co Antrim [8]

A fine Georgian house in the town, now headquarters of a rare daffodil society, was the birthplace of **Alexander Brown** who emigrated in 1800 and founded the first US merchant bank which financed the Baltimore and Ohio Railway.

CAPPAGH, Co Tyrone [25]

Altmore House near Cappagh, now an hotel, was the birthplace in 1806 of **General James Shields** who emigrated in 1826. He defeated General 'Stonewall' Jackson at Kernstown, Virginia.

CARRICKFERGUS, Co Antrim [18]

William of Orange (**William III**) landed here in 1690 before the Battle of the Boyne. In 1778 **Paul Jones**, the American privateer, sailed in and captured the English brig *Drake*.

CASTLETOWN BERE, Co Cork [58]

Dunboy Castle was the last stronghold to hold out for the Spanish after the Battle of Kinsale in 1602.

CASTLEWELLAN, Co Down [34]

Just off the main square is the childhood home of Hollywood star **Greer Garson**. She won an Oscar for her role in the wartime film *Mrs Miniver* which helped boost the British cause in the USA.

CONOGHER near Ballymoney, Co Antrim [2]

The great great grandfather of **President McKinley** (1897–1901) emigrated from here in 1743. The ancestral home was burnt down in 1798 but there is a farm which still bears the McKinley name.

CONG, Co Galway [39]

An abbey town where *The Quiet Man* starring **John Wayne** and **Maureen O'Hara** was filmed.

CRAGGAUNOWEN, near Kilkishen, Co Clare [45]

Here life in pre-Christian Ireland is recreated, and the replica of St Brendan's boat is preserved in a glass house.

DERVOCK, Co Antrim [1]

The grandparents of **W.H. Russell**, founder of the Wild West's Pony Express, emigrated from here.

DOWNPATRICK, Co Down [32]

Cathedral city where **St Patrick** is said to be buried. His gravestone is beside the cathedral.

DUNGIVEN, Co Londonderry [7]

Birthplace of **John McCloskey**, successor in 1864 of Hughes as Archbishop of New York, and the first American Cardinal.

ENNISKILLEN, Co Fermanagh [33]

A marching air of the Royal Inniskilling Fusiliers, who served in America in 1814, is claimed to have become *The Star Spangled Banner*. Documents relating to the claim can be seen in the Regimental Museum.

FOYNES, Co Limerick [46]

The first steamship to sail from this sea port on the Shannon was a blockade runner to the Confederate army in the Civil War. Foynes became the terminus for the seaplane service from America where there is now an aviation museum.

GORTIN, Co Tyrone [20]

Home of the ancestors of **General Sam Houston**, Avenger of the Alamo, who gave his name to the town in Texas.

KINSALE, Co Cork [56]

It was into this haven that the Spanish fleet sailed in 1602 in their attempt to assist the uprising under the Earls of Tyrone and Tyrconnell.

LARNE, Co Antrim [11]

The ferry terminus was once a busy emigration port from where **James Orr**, poet and United Irishman from nearby Ballycarry, fled to America after the 1798 uprising. **President Andrew Johnson**'s grandfather hailed from Mounthill, Larne, and the maternal forebears of **President Theodore Roosevelt** (1901–04) emigrated from Gleno, Larne, in 1729.

LIMAVADY, Co Londonderry [4]

James Monroe, 5th President of the USA, was descended from a family who lived here and took their name from nearby Mount Roe. Here in 1851 **Jane Ross** heard a fiddler playing the tune to which she wrote the words of *The Londonderry Air* (*Danny Boy*).

SBURN, Co Antrim `26`

Christ Church Cathedral a memorial **Lieutenant William Dobbs**, a local an, shows the British and American en-o'-war *Drake* and *Ranger* locked in attle in Belfast Lough during the War of dependence. Dobbs's uncle Arthur ecame Governor of North Carolina. A arble slab depicts the American priva-er **Paul Jones** capturing *Drake* outside arrickfergus harbour in 1778.

SCANNOR, Co Clare `43`

house in Castle Street was the birth-ace of **John P. Holland** (1841–1914), the merican inventor of the submarine.

ONDONDERRY `6`

he home port of the clipper *Minnehaha* hich made three trips a year for 13 years America with emigrants, even during e Civil War. Her crossing time was 15 ays and she made the last scheduled assenger voyage by a sailing ship. Her gurehead is now in the Harbour useum. In 1932 **Amelia Earhart**, the est woman to fly the Atlantic solo, nded in a field on the outskirts of the ty where there is now an interpretive ntre. The ancestors of **Davy Crockett** e said to have hailed from Castlederg, o Tyrone, and emigrated from London-erry. So too did the ancestors of **Stephen oster** in the 18th century. Foster, one of merica's favourite songwriters and omposer of *Beautiful Dreamer*, was born Pennsylvania in 1826.

AGHERA, Co Londonderry `15`

harles Thompson was born here in 29. As Secretary of the first United ates Congress, he read out the *Declara-on of Independence* in 1776.

EWRY, Co Down `35`

ere **Carson**, **Pirie** and **Scott**, founders of e Chicago retail stores, first learnt their usiness. **John Mitchel** (1815–1875), atriot of the Young Ireland movement, turned to Newry after 27 years in exile America and is buried in the Old Meet-g House cemetery. His best known ork is *Jail Journal*. The knee harp, once ayed by pagan bards, is still made here.

PASSAGE EAST, Co Waterford `53`

The port from which SS *Sirius*, the first ship to cross the Atlantic under steam, left for Cobh in 1838 to pick up emigrants for America.

POMEROY, Co Tyrone `23`

The ancestral home of *Apollo* astronaut **James B. Irwin** who drove the first moon buggy in 1971. Two other US astronauts, **Neil Armstrong** and **John Glenn**, are of Ulster stock.

PORTGLENONE, Co Antrim `10`

Timothy Eaton, founder of the Canadian chain store, was an apprentice at D.S. Logan, a general merchant at 48 Main Street, from 1847 to 1852. He worked 16 hours a day and slept under the counter at night. The shop is still trading.

RATHMELTON, Co Donegal `5`

Francis Makemie, founder of the Ameri-can Presbyterian church in 1706, trained for the ministry at the 17th century Meet-ing House, which is now a genealogy centre. The town is on Lough Swilly, from where the Earls of Tyrone and Tyrconnell and their friends fled to France, which was to lead to the plantation of Ulster.

STRABANE, Co Tyrone `12`

There must be many thousands of Ameri-can descendants of the children of Stra-bane Workhouse whose passages across the Atlantic in the early 1840s were paid by the local Board of Guardians. Their old Minutes books give many details of the arrangements made for this 'shovel-ling out'. The town's most famous son is **John Dunlap** who was born at 2 Meeting-house Street in 1747 and served his apprenticeship at Gray's printing shop in Main Street. After emigrating he founded America's first daily newspaper, *The Pennsylvania Packet*, and in 1776 printed the *Declaration of Independence*. **James Wilson**, grandfather of **Woodrow Wilson**, also worked in Gray's printing shop before emigrating in 1807. Other men of Strabane were **Mckeen** and **Thomas Nelson**, signatories of the Decla-ration, **William Knox**, who founded the Central Bank of America, and **J. Ross Stevenson**, Moderator of the General Assembly of the Presbyterian Church

who was of the same Strabane family as Adlai Stevenson.

TIMAHOE, Co Kildare `41`

President Richard Nixon's Milhouse ancestors lie in the Quaker burial ground. The site was visited by him in 1970.

WARRENPOINT, Co Down `36`

This was a busy emigration port, and at nearby Rostrevor `37` an obelisk commemorates Ulsterman **Major General Robert Ross** who captured Washington in 1814, helped himself to dinner prepared for President Madison, drank his best wine and then set fire to the White House.

WATERFORD `50`

A river port where many emigrants started their journey, was founded by the Vikings and became the first town to fall in the Norman invasion of 1170. On display in Reginald's Tower are the uniform and other regalia of American **Brigadier General Thomas Francis Meagher**, founder of the famous Fighting 69th and leader of the Irish Brigade in the battle of Fredericksburg. Meagher was born here in 1823 in what is now the Granville Hotel. He later became Gover-nor of Montana.

WEXFORD `49`

There is a fine monument here to **John Barry** (1745–1803), founder of the US Navy, who was born near Rosslare.

WICKLOW `44`

'The garden of Ireland' and the home town of **Robert C.Halpin**, Captain of the *Great Eastern* which laid the first transat-lantic cable. In the house where he lived the staircase is a facsimile of the main companionway on that ship.

YOUGHAL, Co Cork `54`

Sir Walter Ralegh was once its mayor, and it was here that he smoked the first tobacco and grew the first potatoes in Ireland. His Elizabethan house, Myrtle Grove, although not open to the public, can be seen from the road.

The numbers in the A–Z Tour cross refer to the map on the inside front cover.

ABOVE:
A group of 20th-century Irish emigrants arrive in America to start their new life. There are many sources of information for Irish Americans wishing to trace their roots in Ireland.

Dublin and Belfast are the two main centres for genealogical research, but in recent years many small towns have set up their own local heritage centres, and there are any number of genealogical societies throughout Ireland. Most public libraries can point in the right direction those searching locally for their roots.

Dublin is the location for all of the Republic's centralised records: Births, Deaths and Marriages, Joyce House, 8/11 Lombard Street East, Dublin 2. Most non-Catholic marriages are recorded from 1845, the registration of births, deaths and marriages generally started in 1864.

The National Library in Kildare Street, Dublin 2, houses a major collection of genealogical material, 19th-century trade directories, journals of local historical and archaeological societies, topographical and local histories and most newspapers. It also has on microfilm a collection of pre-1880 Catholic records of baptisms, births and marriages. These give first names and surnames of those listed in each parish register. The Irish Family History Association, c/o The Offaly Historical Society, Tullamore, Co Offaly will supply a list of these registers.

The National Archives, Four Courts, Dublin 1, were badly burnt in 1922, but